Terra ~
Thanks for being
such a great leader!
You make coming to work fun

Happy Birthday
love Stephanie

Great Quotes

FROM

Great Leaders

COMPILED BY

PEGGY ANDERSON

simple truths®
Motivational & Inspirational Gifts
www.simpletruths.com

Published by Simple Truths
1952 McDowell Road, Suite 300
Naperville, IL 60563-65044

Design: Rich Nickel

Printed and bound in the China

ISBN # 978-1-60810-009-5

www.simpletruths.com
(800) 900-3427

06 4CPG 11

TABLE OF CONTENTS

Dedicated with love and gratitude

to my mother Mary

and my stepfather Richard Crisorio.

INTRODUCTION

Throughout history the words of great leaders have inspired,
comforted, persuaded, and motivated.

Regardless of their fields of endeavor, they were all
visionaries who led by example and whose actions
transformed ideas into constructive form.

This collection of timeless wisdom echoes
the integrity, strength of character, and passion of these
extraordinary men and women.

I hope that you will enjoy this book,
and use it as a source of knowledge and inspiration.

Peggy Anderson

Peggy Anderson

Benjamin Franklin

1706-1790

American printer, publisher, author, inventor, scientist and diplomat, Benjamin Franklin is best remembered for his role in separating the American colonies from Great Britain and in helping to frame the Declaration of Independence.

Franklin continued his efforts as an inventor and scientist throughout his diplomatic career, inventing the Franklin stove, bifocal spectacles and the lightning rod. He was the first to institute such public services as a fire department, a lending library, and a learning academy, which later became the University of Pennsylvania.

He served as a delegate to the Second Continental Congress, and then traveled to France to seek military and financial aid for the warring colonies. Franklin was also one of the diplomats chosen to negotiate peace with Britain at war's end, and was instrumental in achieving the adoption of the U.S. Constitution.

"If you desire many things, many things will seem few."

"Lost time is never found again."

"The doors of wisdom are never shut."

*"A house is not a home unless it contains
food and fire for the mind as well as the body."*

*"A man wrapped up in himself
makes a very small bundle."*

*"As we must account for every idle word,
so must we account every idle silence."*

⤳

*"Any society that would give up a little liberty to gain
a little security, will deserve neither and lose both."*

⤳

*"All mankind is divided into three classes:
those that are immoveable,
those that are moveable,
and those that move."*

"An investment in knowledge pays the best interest."

⌇

"Never leave that till tomorrow
which you can do today."

"*Be slow in choosing a friend, slower in changing.*"

"*Half a truth is often a great lie.*"

"*He does not possess wealth; it possesses him.*"

"*Life's tragedy is that we get old too soon and wise too late.*"

"Rather go to bed without dinner than to rise in debt."

~

"Take time for all things: great haste makes great waste."

~

"The discontented man finds no easy chair."

~

"Well done is better than well said."

~

"Words may show a man's wit but actions his meaning."

Winston Churchill
1874-1965

Sir Winston Churchill — author, orator and statesman — led Great Britain from the brink of defeat to victory as wartime prime minister. Born in Oxfordshire, England in 1874, Churchill began serving his country as a military leader in World War I. As a member of Parliament, his repeated warnings of the menace of Hitler's Germany, combined with his aggressive and convincing oratory skills, resulted in his appointment to prime minister in 1939.

He joined Franklin D. Roosevelt and Joseph Stalin in 1940 to shape Allied strategy in World War II. An intense patriot and romantic believer in his country's greatness, Churchill gave his people the strong leadership and devotion that ultimately led to Britain's military salvation.

He was awarded the Nobel Prize for literature in 1953 for his book, *The Second World War*, and also was knighted the same year.

"I have nothing to offer but blood, toil, tears, and sweat."

"A lie gets halfway around the world before
the truth has a chance to put its pants on."

～

"Courage is going from failure to failure
without losing enthusiasm."

～

"Success is not final, failure is not fatal:
it is the courage to continue that counts."

～

"If we are together nothing is impossible."
If we are divided all will fail."

"Never give in .. never, never, never,
never, in nothing great or small,
large or petty, never give in except to
convictions of honor and good sense."

~

"The price of greatness is responsibility."

~

"All great things are simple and
many can be expressed in single words:
freedom, justice, honor, duty,
mercy, hope."

"Every day you may make progress. Every step may be fruitful. Yet there will stretch out before you an ever-lengthening, ever-ascending, ever-improving path. You know you will never get to the end of the journey. But this, so far from discouraging, only adds to the joy and glory of the climb."

"We make a living by what we get.
We make a life by what we give."

⌇

"It is a mistake to look too far ahead.
Only one link in the chain of destiny
can be handled at a time."

⌇

"To build may have to be the slow and laborious task of years.
To destroy can be the thoughtless act of a single day."

"Difficulties mastered are opportunities won."

"It's not enough that we do our best; sometimes we have to do what's required."

"I never worry about action, only inaction."

"Courage is the finest of human qualities because it guarantees all the others."

Thomas Jefferson

1743-1826

The third President of the United States and its first secretary of state, Thomas Jefferson is best remembered as the principal author of the Declaration of Independence.

A wealthy Virginia planter, Jefferson began his political career as a member of the House of Burgesses in 1769. Later, as a delegate to the Second Continental Congress, he was appointed along with Benjamin Franklin and John Adams to draft a formal statement of reasons for separation from Great Britain. The resultant Declaration of Independence, largely penned by Jefferson, summed up the commitment of the young country to life, liberty and self-government.

He went on to serve as the U.S. minister in France before accepting George Washington's appointment as the first secretary of state. Assuming the Presidency in 1801, he soon doubled the size of the United States with the purchase of the Louisiana Territory from Napoleon. He devoted his life in retirement to establishing the University of Virginia.

"The boisterous sea of liberty is never without a wave."

"The will of the people is the only legitimate foundation of any government, and to protect its free expression should be our first object."

～

"Delay is preferable to error."

～

"Determine never to be idle... It is wonderful much may be done if we are always doing."

"It is neither wealth nor splendor, but tranquility and occupation which give happiness."

∾

"An honest man can feel no pleasure in exercise of power over his fellow citizens."

∾

"We hold these truths to be self-evident: That all men are created equal; that they are endowed by their Creator with certain unalienable rights; that among these are life, liberty, and the pursuit of happiness."

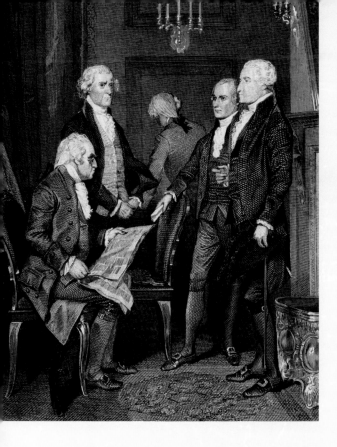

"We do not raise armies for glory or for conquest."

∽

"A coward is much more exposed to quarrels than a man of spirit."

∽

"For here we are not afraid to follow truth wherever it may lead."

"The government is the strongest of which every man feels a part."

∽

"Nothing can stop the man with the right mental attitude from achieving his goal; nothing on earth can help a man with the wrong mental attitude."

∽

"There is not a truth existing which I fear … or would wish unknown to the whole world."

*"Whenever you do a thing,
act as if all the world
were watching."*

∽

*"When you reach the end of your
rope, tie a knot in it and hang on."*

Mother Teresa

1910–1997

Mother Teresa, born Agnes Gonxha Bojarhiu, is revered for her lifelong dedication to the poor, most notably the destitute masses of India.

In 1928, at the age of 18, she went to Ireland to join the Institute of the Blessed Virgin Mary and shortly thereafter traveled to India to work with the poor of Calcutta. After studying nursing, she moved into the slums of the city where she founded the Order of the Missionaries of Charity. Mother Teresa was summoned to Rome in 1968 to find a home for the needy, and three years later she was awarded the first Pope John XXIII Peace Prize.

By the late 1970's, the Missionaries of Charity numbered more than 1,000 nuns who operated 60 centers in Calcutta and more than 200 centers worldwide. Her selfless commitment to helping the poor saved the lives of nearly 8,000 people in Calcutta alone. Mother Teresa's compassion and devotion to the destitute earned her the Nobel Peace Prize in 1979.

"Kind words can be short and easy to speak, but their echoes are truly endless."

"Be faithful in small things because it is in them that your strength lies."

"Do not wait for leaders; do it alone, person to person."

"I have found the paradox, that if you love until it hurts, there can be no more hurt."

"Good works are links that form a chain of love."

"If we have no peace, it is because we have forgotten that we belong to each other."

~

"If we want a love message to be heard, it has got to be sent out. To keep a lamp burning, we have to keep putting oil in it."

"If you can't feed a hundred people, then feed just one."

"If you judge people, you have no time to love them."

∽

"In this life we cannot do great things.
We can only do small things with great love."

∽

"Intense love does not measure, it just gives."

∽

"Joy is a net of love by which you can catch souls."

*"Let us always meet each other with a smile,
for the smile is the beginning of love."*

*"Love is a fruit in season at all times,
and within reach of every hand."*

*"We ourselves feel that what we are doing is just a drop
in the ocean. But the ocean would be less because
of missing that drop."*

"We shall never know all the good that a simple smile can do."

⤳

"Words which do not give the light of Christ increase the darkness."

George Washington
1732-1799

American general, commander-in-chief of the colonial armies in the American Revolution and subsequently the first President of the United States, George Washington became known as the father of his country.

Born into a wealthy family of Virginia planters, Washington worked as a surveyor and gained military experience in the French and Indian War. The impending American Revolution would call him to his country's aid.

Washington was named commander-in-chief of the military force of all the colonies in 1775. Over the next five years, including the nadir of the harsh winter at Valley Forge, Washington held the American forces together by sheer strength of character. His capture of Cornwallis at Yorktown in 1781 marked the end of the war.

Alone commanding the respect of both parties, Washington was chosen unanimously to preside over the Constitutional Convention. He was elected the country's first President in 1789 and re-elected four years later.

"Labor to keep alive in your breast that little spark of celestial fire, called conscience."

G Washington

"A slender acquaintance with the world must convince every man that actions, not words, are the true criterion of the attachment of friends."

〜

"Associate with men of good quality if you esteem your own reputation; for it is better to be alone than in bad company."

〜

"Be courteous to all, but intimate with few, and let those few be well tried before you give them your confidence."

*"Few men have virtue to withstand
the highest bidder."*

∽

*"I hope I shall possess firmness and virtue enough
to maintain what I consider the most enviable of all titles,
the character of an honest man."*

∽

*"Friendship is a plant of slow growth and
must undergo and withstand the shocks of
adversity before it is entitled to the
appellation."*

"Happiness and moral duty are inseparably connected."

∽

"If the freedom of speech is taken away then dumb and silent we may be led, like sheep to the slaughter."

"Let your heart feel for the afflictions and distress of everyone, and let your hand give in proportion to your purse."

~

"It is better to offer no excuse than a bad one."

~

"Liberty, when it begins to take root, is a plant of rapid growth."

"To be prepared for war is one of the most effective means of preserving peace."

∽

"Truth will ultimately prevail where there are pains to bring it to light."

"Worry is the interest paid by those who borrow trouble."

Martin
Luther King, Jr.

1929–1968

Martin Luther King, Jr. used his strong personality and eloquent oratory to spearhead the civil rights movement in the United States during the 1950's and 1960's. A Baptist minister, King began his civil rights activities in 1955 with the successful boycott of the segregated bus system in Montgomery, Alabama.

He founded the Southern Christian Leadership Conference in 1957 in an effort to mobilize the nonviolent struggle against racism and discrimination. On August 28, 1963, the massive "March on Washington" culminated in 200,000 Americans of all races gathering at the Lincoln Memorial to hear King speak.

The movement won a major victory in 1964 when Congress passed the Civil Rights Act, and King became the youngest man ever to receive the Nobel Peace Prize. The world lost a towering symbol of liberty and justice when an assassin's bullet claimed his life in 1968.

"The time is always right to do what is right."

36

*"Human progress is neither automatic nor inevitable ...
Every step toward the goal of justice requires sacrifice,
suffering, and struggle; the tireless exertions and
passionate concern of dedicated individuals."*

∽

*"I have a dream that one day this nation will rise up
and live out the true meaning of this creed —
We hold these truths to be self-evident:
that all men are created equal."*

∽

*"History will have to record that the greatest tragedy
of this period ... was not the strident clamor of the bad
people, but the appalling silence of the good people."*

"It is not possible to be in favor of justice for some people and not be in favor of justice for all people."

"Faith is taking the first step even when you don't see the staircase."

"The ultimate measure of a man is not where he stands in moments of comfort and convenience, but where he stands at times of challenge and controversy."

"A lie cannot live."

"Love is the only force capable of transforming an enemy to a friend."

"The quality, not the longevity, of one's life is what is important."

"*War is a poor chisel to carve out tomorrow.*"

∿

"*We must learn to live together as brothers
or perish together as fools.*"

∿

"*Every person must decide whether
to walk in the light of creative altruism
or in the darkness of destructive selfishness.
This is the judgment. Life's most persistent
and urgent question is, what are
you doing for others?*"

"A just law is a man-made code that squares with the moral law or the law of God."

"Now is the time to make justice a reality for all of God's children."

"I believe the unarmed truth and unconditional love will have the final word in reality."

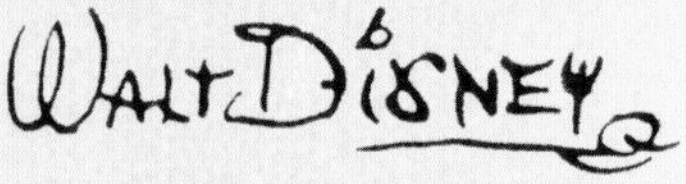

Walt Disney

1901-1966

Walt Disney, the pioneer of animated cartoon films, displayed his creative talents at an early age. His interest in art led him to study cartooning through a correspondence school, and he later took classes at the Kansas City Art Institute and School of Design.

In the late 1920's, Disney recognized the potential for sound in cartoon films. He produced "Steamboat Willie", a cartoon short equipped with voices and music, and the character of Mickey Mouse was introduced to the public.

During the economic hard times of the 1930's, Disney's cartoons captivated his audiences. His body of work firmly established him as the unparalleled master of feature-length animated films.

Walt Disney was the recipient of 48 Academy Awards and 7 Emmys. His creativity, ingenuity and ability to bring his fantasies to fruition continue to enchant all ages.

"If you can dream it, you can do it."

～

"All the adversity I've had in my life, all my troubles have strengthened me ... You may not realize it when it happens, but a kick in the teeth may be the best thing in the world for you."

～

"When you believe in a thing, believe in it all the way, implicitly and unquestionable."

"*The way to get started is to quit talking and begin doing.*"

∾

"*Our greatest natural resource is the minds of our children.*"

∾

"*It's kind of fun to do the impossible.*"

∾

"*Our heritage and ideals, our codes and standards — the things we live by and teach our children - are preserved or diminished by how freely we exchange ideas and feelings.*"

"We keep moving forward, opening new doors, and doing things, because we're curious and curiosity keeps leading to new paths."

"Disneyland will never be completed. It will continue to grow as long as there is imagination left in the world."

Abraham Lincoln

1809-1865

The 16th President of the United States, Abraham Lincoln preserved the Union during the American Civil War. Lincoln's inner qualities of faithfulness, honesty, resolution, humor and courage gave him the strength to lead his country during the bloodiest years of its existence.

Born in the backwoods of Kentucky, in 1809, Lincoln worked as a rail splitter, flatboatman, storekeeper, postmaster and surveyor before becoming a lawyer. His debates while running for the Senate made him a nationally known figure, and he was elected President in 1860.

By the time Lincoln had taken office, seven states already had seceded from the Union over the issue of slavery. Lincoln issued his Emancipation Proclamation in 1863 to set the slaves in the rebellious states free. He coordinated every aspect of the war effort as commander-in-chief, and his military genius was instrumental in the Union victory. Re-elected in 1864, Lincoln was tragically assassinated before he could oversee the Reconstruction of the South.

"The best thing about the future is that it comes only one day at a time."

Abraham Lincoln

"*Those who deny freedom to others, deserve it not for themselves; and , under a just God, can not long retain it.*"

~

"*Let us have faith that right makes might, and that faith, let us, to the end, dare to do our duty as we understand it.*"

~

"*I leave you hoping that the lamp of liberty will burn in your bosoms until there shall no longer be a doubt that all men are created free and equal.*"

"*Fourscore and seven years ago our Fathers brought forth on this continent a new nation, conceived in liberty and dedicated to the proposition that all men are created equal.*"

"*Leave nothing for tomorrow which can be done today.*"

"*Force is all-conquering, but its victories are short-lived.*"

"Stand with anybody that stands right. Stand with him while he is right and part with him when he goes wrong."

∽

"The probability that we may fall in the struggle ought not to deter us from the support of a cause we believe to be just."

"A house divided against itself cannot stand."

"I am rather inclined to silence, and whether that be wise or not, it is at least more unusual nowadays to find a man who can hold his tongue than to find one who cannot."

"The man does not live who is more devoted to peace than I am. None who would do more to preserve it."

⌇

"I do not think much of a man who is not wiser today than he was yesterday."

⌇

"As I would not be a slave, so I would not be a master. This expresses my idea of democracy. Whatever differs from this, to the extent of the difference, is no democracy."

Vince Lombardi

1913-1970

Professional football coach Vince Lombardi became a national symbol of single-minded determination to win. In nine seasons as the head coach of the previously moribund Green Bay Packers, Lombardi led the team to five NFL championships and to victory in the first two Super Bowls.

At Fordham University, Lombardi played guard on the famous line known as the "Seven Blocks of Granite". He studied law at Fordham and had a brief career as a minor league football player before becoming a high school coach in 1939. After serving as an assistant coach in college and in the pros, he was hired as head coach and general manager of the Green Bay Packers in 1959. His Spartan training regimen and personal drive turned the Green Bay Packers from a team accustomed to defeat to the paragon of victory.

He went on to become head coach, general manager and part owner of the Washington Redskins before dying of cancer in 1970.

*"Winning is not a sometime thing.
You don't do things right
once in a while ...
you do them right all the time."*

Vince Lombardi

"There is only one way to succeed in anything,
and that is to give it everything.
I do, and I demand that my players do."

~

"Confidence is contagious. So is the lack of confidence."

~

"Leaders aren't born, they are made. They are made
by hard effort, which is the price which all of us
must pay to achieve any goal which is worthwhile."

~

"Once you learn to quit, it becomes a habit."

"The price of success is hard work, dedication to the job and the determination that whether we win or lose, we have applied the best of ourselves to the task at hand."

"The only place success comes before work is in the dictionary."

"The greatest accomplishment is not in never falling, but in rising after you fall."

"Winners never quit and quitters never win."

"Individual commitment to a group effort — that is what makes a team work, a company work, a society work, a civilization work."

"The quality of a person's life is in direct proportion to their commitment to excellence, regardless of their chosen field of endeavor."

"Man's finest hour is the moment when he has worked his heart out in a good cause and lies exhausted on the field of battle victorious."

"The difference between a successful person and others is not a lack of strength, not a lack of knowledge, but rather in a lack of will."

"Mental toughness is many things and rather difficult to explain. Its qualities are sacrifice and self-denial."

"Once you have established the goal you want and the price you're willing to pay, you can ignore the minor hurts, the opponent's pressure and the temporary failures."

~

"Some of us will do our jobs well and some will not, but we will all be judged on one thing: the result."

Eleanor Roosevelt

1884–1962

Eleanor Roosevelt was a United Nations diplomat, humanitarian and wife of President Franklin D. Roosevelt.

During her twelve years as First Lady (1933 – 1945), the unprecedented breadth of her activities and advocacy of liberal causes made her nearly as controversial a figure as her husband. Roosevelt instituted regular White House press conferences for women correspondents for the first time. In deference to the President's illness, she helped serve as his "eyes and ears" throughout the nation, embarking on extensive tours around the country. She showed particular interest in such humanitarian concerns as child welfare, slum clearance projects and equal rights.

After President Roosevelt's death (1945), President Harry Truman appointed her as a delegate to the United Nations, where, as chairman of the UN Commission on Human Rights, she played a major role in the drafting and adoption of the Universal Declaration of Human Rights.

Eleanor Roosevelt was one of the most widely admired women in the world and remains an inspiration to many.

"The future belongs to those who believe in the beauty of their dreams."

"Absence makes the heart grow fonder."

～

"Happiness is not a goal; it is a by-product."

～

"Friendship with ones self is all important, because without it one cannot be friends with anyone else in the world."

*"In the long run, we shape our lives,
and we shape ourselves. The process never
ends until we die. And the choices we make
are ultimately our own responsibility."*

"It is better to light a candle than curse the darkness."

*"It isn't enough to talk about peace.
One must believe in it.
And it isn't enough to believe in it.
One must work at it."*

*"Justice cannot be
for one side alone,
but must be for
both."*

~

*"No one can make
you feel inferior
without your
consent."*

~

"Only a man's character is the real criterion of worth."

"The giving of love is an education in itself."

⤴

"We gain strength, and courage, and confidence by each experience in which we really stop to look fear in the face... we must do that which we think we cannot."

"What is to give light must
endure the burning."

～

"When you cease to make a contribution, you begin to die."

～

"Women are like teabags.
We don't know our true strength
until we are in hot water!"

Dwight Eisenhower

1890-1969

It was a blend of honesty, humility and persistence that marked Dwight D. Eisenhower's success as both the 34th President of the United States and as the supreme commander of the Allied forces during World War II.

Eisenhower graduated from West Point and commanded a tank training center during World War I. At the outbreak of World War II, Eisenhower was appointed to the Army's war plans division, where he prepared strategy for the Allied invasion of Europe. He was later selected commander of U.S. troops in Europe.

He retired to become President of Columbia University and publish his best-selling account of the war. Wooed by both parties, Eisenhower ran as a Republican for President in 1952 and 1956, winning both times. Eisenhower enjoyed tremendous popularity with the American people, and worked to expand Social Security and increase the minimum wage. In addition, he created the Department of Health, Education and Welfare and NASA.

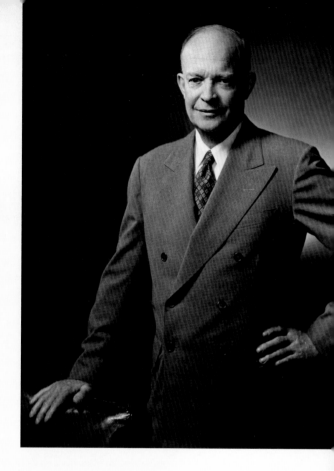

"A people that values its privileges above its principles soon loses both.

*"The final battle against intolerance is to be fought —
not in the chambers of any legislature — but in the
hearts of men."*

∽

*"When you are in any contest you should work as if there were,
to the very last minute, a chance to lose it."*

∽

*"The supreme quality for leadership is unquestionable
integrity. Without it, no real success is possible."*

"Only strength can cooperate. Weakness can only beg."

⌒

"Pessimism never won any battle."

"You don't lead by hitting people over the head — that's assault, not leadership."

⌒

"Only our individual faith in freedom can keep us free."

"A sense of humor is part of the art of leadership,
  of getting along with people, of getting things done."

~

"May we grow in strength — without pride of self.
  May we, in our dealings with all people of the earth
  speak the truth and serve justice. May the light
  of freedom, coming to all darkened lands, flame brightly
  — until at last the darkness is no more."

~

"The history of freedom is never really
  written by chance but by choice."

Nelson Mandela
1918–

Nelson Rolihlahla Mandela was the first President of South Africa to be elected in fully-representative democratic elections. He joined the African National Congress, ANC, in 1944 and was an anti-apartheid activist. Mandela was imprisoned for plotting to overthrow the government to end apartheid.

Throughout his 27 years in prison, Nelson Mandela rejected any compromise of his political position to procure his freedom. Upon his release in 1990, Mandela proclaimed his commitment to reconciliation and peace with the country's white minority. During his presidency from 1994-1999 he oversaw the transition from minority rule and apartheid.

After retirement Mandela became an advocate for numerous social and human rights organizations. He has been honored with more than a hundred awards in recognition of his tireless dedication and contribution to these causes. Nelson Mandela's strong ideals of international understanding and peace continue to impact the world.

"The greatest glory in living lies not in never falling, but in rising every time we fall."

Mandela

"As we let our own light shine, we unconsciously give other people permission to do the same."

∽

"For to be free is not merely to cast off one's chains, but to live in a way that respects and enhances the freedom of others."

∽

"Education is the most powerful weapon which you can use to change the world."

∽

"True reconciliation does not consist in merely forgetting the past."

"After climbing a great hill, one only finds that there are many more hills to climb."

❧

"Man's goodness is a flame that can be hidden but never extinguished."

❧

*"The first thing is to be honest with yourself. You can never have an impact on society if you have not changed yourself…
Great peacemakers are all people of integrity, of honesty, and humility."*

"The brave man is not he who does not feel afraid, but he who conquers that fear."

〜

"No one is born hating another person because of the color of his skin, or his background, or his religion. People must learn to hate, and if they can learn to hate, they can be taught to love, for love comes more naturally to the human heart than its opposite."

〜

"A good head and a good heart are always a formidable combination."

"There is no passion to be found playing small — in settling for a life that is less than the one you are capable of living."

"Leaders are important but history is ultimately not made by kings and generals. It is made by the masses."

"I have cherished the ideal of a democratic
and free society in which all persons live together
in harmony and with equal opportunities.
It is an ideal which I hope to live for and to
achieve. But if needs be, it is an ideal
for which I am prepared to die."

"We can't afford to stand divided ... If we stand together,
victory of the liberation movement is assured."

"There can be no keener revelation of a society's
soul than the way in which it treats its children."

Albert Einstein
1879-1955

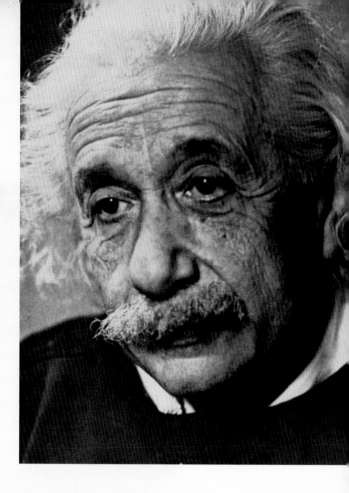

One of the greatest scientific minds of all time, Albert Einstein is best known for his contributions to the field of physics. Born in Germany in 1879, Einstein received his diploma from the Swiss Federal Polytechnic School in Zurich, where he trained as a teacher in physics and mathematics. In 1905, he received his Ph.D. and published four research papers, the most significant being the creation of the special theory of relativity. He became internationally famous when he was awarded the Nobel Prize for Physics in 1922.

The important military implications of the discovery of the fission of uranium in 1939 led Einstein to appeal to President Franklin Roosevelt. Einstein's letter to the president led to the development of the atomic bomb.

Einstein left the field of physics greatly changed through his brilliant contributions. His discoveries provided the impetus for future research into understanding the mysteries of the universe.

"Imagination is more important than knowledge."

Albert Einstein.

"The ideals which have lighted my way, and time after time have given me new courage to face life cheerfully, have been kindness, beauty, and truth."

～

"Truth is what stands the test of experience."

～

"The important thing is not to stop questioning. Curiosity has its own reason for existing. One cannot help but be in awe when he contemplates the mysteries of eternity, of life, of the marvelous structure of reality. It is enough if one tries merely to comprehend a little of this mystery every day. Never lose a holy curiosity."

"Try not to become a man of success but rather to become a man of value."

"If you are out to describe the truth, leave elegance to the tailor."

"The most important human endeavor is the striving for morality in our action. Our inner balances and even our very existence depend on it. Only morality in our actions can give beauty and dignity to life."

"When I examined myself, and my methods of thought, I came to the conclusion that the gift of fantasy has meant more to me than my talent for absorbing positive knowledge."

"A person who never made a mistake never tried anything new."

"Weakness of attitude becomes weakness of character."

"Whoever is careless with the truth in small matters cannot be trusted with important matters."

"*The only real valuable thing is intuition.*"

~

"*We can't solve problems by using the same kind of thinking we used when we created them.*"

~

"*There are only two ways to live your life.*
One is as though nothing is a miracle.
The other is as though everything is a miracle."

"Intellectuals solve problems, geniuses prevent them."

"Information is not knowledge."

"The intuitive mind is a sacred gift and the rational mind is a faithful servant. We have created a society that honors the servant and has forgotten the gift."

John F. Kennedy
1917-1963

John F. Kennedy was elected the 35th President of the United States at the age of 43 — the youngest man and first Roman Catholic ever elected.

Kennedy graduated from Harvard University in 1936 and joined the U.S. Navy shortly before World War II. While on active duty in the Pacific, the Japanese destroyed the boat under his command, PT 109. Despite a back injury, Kennedy showed great heroism in rescuing his crew.

After holding seats in both the House and Senate, Kennedy was elected President in 1960. His style, charisma and oratory won him admiration at home and abroad, but his life was tragically cut short by an assassin's bullet in 1963. His major accomplishments include the formation of the Peace Corps and his deft handling of the Cuban Missile Crisis. His book, *Profiles in Courage,* won the Pulitzer Prize in 1957.

"We need men who can dream of things that never were."

"The American, by nature, is optimistic. He is experimental, an inventor and a builder who builds best when called upon to build greatly."

❧

"Those who dare to fail miserably can achieve greatly."

❧

"We stand for freedom. That is our conviction for ourselves; that is our only commitment to others."

"My fellow Americans, ask not what your country can do for you, ask what you can do for your country."

"There are risks and costs to a program of action. But they are far less than the long-range risks and costs of comfortable inaction."

"Do not pray for easy lives. Pray to be stronger men."

"Liberty without learning is always in peril;
learning without liberty is always in vain."

❧

"A man may die, nations may rise and fall, but an idea lives forever."

❧

"Victory has a thousand fathers,
but defeat is an orphan."

❧

"Change is the law of life.
Those who look only to the past or the present
are certain to miss the future."

Mahatma Gandhi
1869-1948

Leader of the Indian Nationalist movement against British rule, Mohandas "Mahatma" Gandhi is revered as the father of his country. He is esteemed internationally for his doctrine of nonviolence to achieve political and social progress.

Gandhi received an education in India before beginning law studies in England in 1888. Seeking clerical work in South Africa, he was shocked at the racial discrimination he encountered. He became an advocate for his fellow Indians, and his challenges to the government resulted in a jail sentence.

He entered politics in India in 1919 to protest British sedition laws. He emerged as the head of the Indian National Congress, where he advocated a policy of nonviolent protest to achieve Indian independence. Repressed throughout World War II, Gandhi successfully negotiated for an autonomous Indian state in 1947. He was assassinated one year later.

"Happiness is when what you think, what you say, and what you do are in harmony."

M K Gandhi

"*A coward is incapable of exhibiting love;
it is the prerogative of the brave.*"

﹏

"*A man is but the product of his thoughts. What he thinks, he becomes.*"

﹏

"*Nonviolence is not a garment to be put on
and off at will. Its seat is in the heart, and it
must be an inseparable part of our being.*"

﹏

"*Live as if you were to die tomorrow.
Learn as if you were to live forever.*"

"We must become the change
we want to see in the world."

⌒

"Power is of two kinds. One is obtained by the fear of
punishment and the other by acts of love. Power based on love
is a thousand times more effective and permanent than the one
derived from fear of punishment."

⌒

"Glory lies in the attempt to reach
one's goal and not in reaching it."

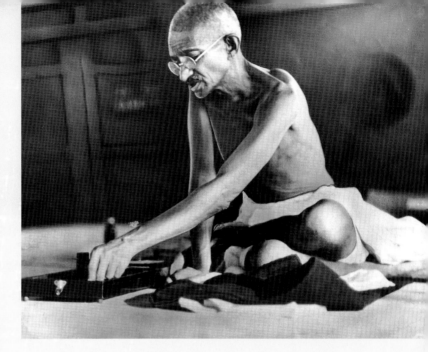

*"An ounce of practice
is worth more than
tons of preaching."*

"An eye for an eye ends up making the whole world blind."

*"Love never claims, it ever gives.
Love ever suffers, never resents
never revenges itself."*

Helen Keller

1880-1968

Helen Adams Keller was born in Tuscumbia, Alabama, in 1880. She was deprived of sight, hearing and the ability to speak before the age of two due to a severe illness. Her life represents one of the most extraordinary examples of a person who was able to transcend her physical handicaps.

Through the constant and patient instruction of Anne Sullivan, Helen Keller not only learned to read, write and speak, but went on to graduate *cum laude* from Radcliffe College in 1904.

As well as becoming the author of several articles, books and biographies, she was active on the staffs of the American Foundation for the Blind and the American Foundation for the Overseas Blind. She also lectured in more than 25 countries and received several awards of great distinction.

Helen Keller's courage, faith and optimism in the face of such overwhelming disabilities had a profound effect on all she touched. Her tremendous accomplishments stand as a symbol of the potential in all of us.

"To be blind, but worse is to have eyes and not see."

HeLen KeLLer

"When one door of happiness closes,
another opens; but often we look so long
at the closed door that we do not see
the one which has been opened for us."

&

"Happiness cannot come from without.
It must come from within."

&

"What we have once enjoyed we
can never lose. All that we love deeply
becomes a part of us."

"We would never learn to be brave and patient if there were only joy in the world."

~

"The struggle of life is one of our greatest blessings.
It makes us patient, sensitive, and Godlike.
It teaches us that although the world is full of suffering,
it is also full of the overcoming of it."

~

"The best and most beautiful things in life
cannot be seen, not touched, but are
felt in the heart."

"Character cannot be developed in ease and quiet.
Only through experiences of trial and suffering
can the soul be strengthened, vision cleared,
ambition inspired and success achieved."

Henry Ford

1863-1947

Celebrated as both a technological genius and a folk hero, Henry Ford was the creative force in the automotive industry. His innovations changed the economic and social character of his country — and the world.

Ford developed the mass-produced "Model T" automobile and sold it at a price the average person could afford. Use of the assembly line in mass production saved time and money and allowed Ford to offer more cars to the American public at a lower price than anyone before him. More than 15 million "Model T's" were sold in the United States between 1908 and 1927.

A noted philanthropist, Ford established Greenfield Village, a group of historical buildings and landmarks in Dearborn, Michigan. He also established the Henry Ford Museum and the Ford Foundation.

"Anybody can do anything that he imagines."

Henry Ford

"*Quality means doing it right
when no one is looking.*"

⌐

"*When everything seems to be going against you, remember
that the airplane takes off against the wind, not with it.*"

⌐

"*A business that makes nothing but money
is a poor kind of business.*"

⌐

"*Failure is simply the opportunity to
begin again more intelligently.*"

"Chop your own wood,
  and it will warm you twice."

"Before everything else,
  getting ready is the secret
  of success."

"Obstacles are those frightful things you see
  when you take your eyes off your goal."

*"Everything comes to him who
hustles while he waits."*

∽

*"If everyone is moving forward together,
then success will take care of itself."*

∽

*"Most people spend more time and energy
going around problems than trying to solve them."*

∽

*"I cannot discover that anyone knows enough to
say definitely what is and what is not possible."*

"Wealth, like happiness, is never attained when sought after directly. It comes as a by product of providing a useful service."

"You can't build a reputation on what you're going to do."

"Coming together is a beginning.
Keeping together is progress.
Working together is success."

"Life is a series of experiences, each of which makes us bigger, even though it is hard to realize this. For the world was built to develop character, and we must learn that the setbacks and griefs which we endure help us in our marching onward."

Ronald Reagan

1911-2004

The 40th President of the United States, Ronald Reagan was dubbed "The Great Communicator". He has been credited with restoring optimism to the American people and being instrumental in the 1991 downfall of the Soviet Union.

Reagan was known for his ability to convey ideas in a persuasive and well-delivered speaking style. He shifted from the Democratic Party affiliation and moved into Republican politics. During his presidency he sustained an adversarial approach to the USSR. Reagan made the abolition of communism and the implementation of supply-side economics the primary focus of his time in office.

Throughout the duration of his term as President, Reagan was committed to the ideologies of democratic capitalism. He departed from the office immensely popular, and of Americans polled, 87% choose Ronald Reagan as one of the most popular United States Presidents.

"I know in my heart that man is good. That what is right will eventually triumph. And there is purpose and worth to each and every life."

Ronald Reagan

"Freedom is a fragile thing and is never more than one generation from extinction. It is not ours by inheritance; it must be fought for and defended constantly by each generation, for it comes only once to a people. Those who have known freedom, and then lost it, have never known it again."

~

"There are no easy answers ... but there are simple answers. We must have the courage to do what we know is morally right."

~

"There are no such things as limits to growth, because there are no limits to the human capacity for intelligence, imagination, and wonder."

"A man is not free unless government is limited."

~

"We can't help everyone, but everyone can help someone."

~

"Entrepreneurs and their small enterprises are responsible for almost all the economic growth in the United States."

~

"Freedom is one of the deepest and noblest aspirations of the human spirit."

*"America is
too great
for small
dreams."*

*"Peace is not the absence of conflict, it is the
ability to handle conflict by peaceful means."*

*"We will always remember. We will always be proud.
We will always be prepared, so we will always be free."*

"*The best minds are not in government.
If any were, business would hire them away.*"

⌒

"*Life is one grand, sweet song, so start the music.*"

⌒

"*I'm convinced more than ever that man finds
liberation only when he binds himself to God
and commits himself to his fellow man.*"

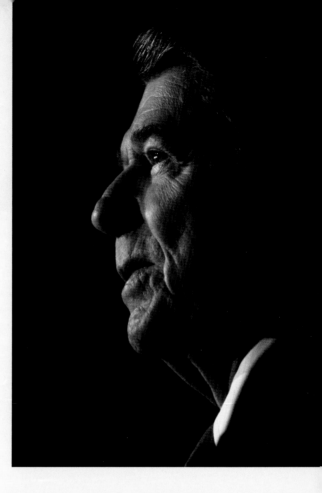

"Recession is when a neighbor loses his job. Depression is when you lose yours."

∽

"They say the world has become too complex for simple answers. They are wrong."

∽

"Our forbearance should never be misunderstood. Our reluctance for conflict should not be misjudged as failure of will. When action is required to preserve our national security, we will act."

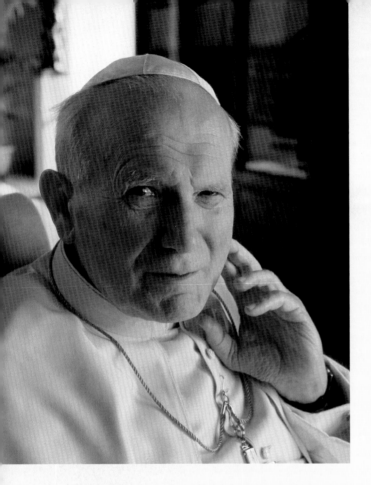

Pope John Paul II
1920–2005

When Pope John Paul II was invested in 1978, he became the first Polish pope in the Church's history — and the first non-Italian pope in 456 years. This remarkable man has encompassed the globe to bring the doctrine of the Catholic Church to the world's people.

Born Karol Wojtyla in Wadowice, Poland, he studied Polish literature and worked in a chemical factory before the outbreak of World War II. Determined to become a priest, he went into hiding at the palace of the archbishop of Krakow and was ordained in 1946. He later became archbishop of Krakow after receiving a doctorate in ethics and becoming a professor of philosophy. He was made cardinal in 1967 and elected pope just over 10 years later.

His fluency in a number of languages uniquely qualified him as an international ambassador for the Church. His passionate commitment to spread the Word of God continued until his death in 2005.

"The future starts today, not tomorrow."

Joannes Paulus pp II

*"Anything done for another
is done for oneself."*

⁝

*"Peace is not just the absence of war.
Like a cathedral, peace must be
constructed patiently and with
unshakable faith."*

⁝

*"The truth is not always the same
as the majority decision."*

"The worst prison would be a closed heart."

∾

"The only way to peace is forgiveness.
To accept and give forgiveness makes possible
a new quality of rapport between men,
interrupts the spiral of hatred and revenge
and breaks the chains of evil
which bind the hearts of rivals."

∾

"Love is never defeated."

*"Freedom consists not in doing what we like,
but in having the right to do what we ought."*

Franklin Roosevelt

1882-1945

The 32nd President of the United States, Franklin Delano Roosevelt served for more than 12 years, longer than any other man. He greatly expanded federal powers to affect economic recovery during the Great Depression and was a major Allied leader during World War II.

Roosevelt attended Harvard University and the Columbia University School of Law. He was elected to the New York Senate in 1910 and became assistant secretary of the Navy three years later. He remained active in Democratic politics despite being stricken by polio and was elected governor of New York in 1928.

Elected President in 1931, Roosevelt quickly obtained passage of a sweeping economic program, the New Deal which provided relief, loans and jobs through a variety of federal agencies. Roosevelt mobilized industry for military production and extended aid to Great Britain. He played a leading role in creating the alliance with Britain and the U.S.S.R. that led to victory in World War II.

"To reach a port, we must sail — sail, not tie at anchor — sail, not drift."

Franklin D Roosevelt

"Confidence...thrives on honesty, on honor, on the sacredness of obligations, on faithful protection and on unselfish performance. Without them it cannot live."

"Happiness lies in the joy of achievement and the thrill of creative effort."

"Human kindness has never weakened the stamina or softened the fiber of a free people. A nation does not have to be cruel to be tough."

"*I'm not the smartest fellow in the world,
but I can sure pick smart colleagues.*"

～

"*Rules are not necessarily sacred, principles are.*"

～

"*If civilization is to survive, we must cultivate the science
of human relationships — the ability of all peoples, of
all kinds, to live together, in the same world at peace.*"

～

"*In our seeking for economic and political progress, we
all go up — or else we all go down.*"

"Men are not prisoners of fate, but only prisoners of their own minds."

"Physical strength can never permanently withstand the impact of spiritual force."

"The only limit to our realization of tomorrow will be our doubts of today."

"The only thing we have to fear is fear itself."

"The virtues are lost in self-interest
as rivers are lost in the sea."

"There are many ways of going forward,
but only one way of standing still."

"The truth is found when men are
free to pursue it."

"The test of our progress is not whether we add more to the abundance of those who have much; it is whether we provide enough for those who have too little."

"We and all others who believe in freedom as deeply as we do, would rather die on our feet than live on our knees."

George S. Patton

1885-1945

Relentless, hard-driving and tenacious are only a few adjectives to describe George S. Patton Jr., one of the foremost American combat generals of World War II. He was the chief proponent of the adoption of mobile weapons and armored vehicles, and his bravery as a tank commander played a major role in halting the German counterattack at the Battle of the Bulge.

His ruthless sweep across France in the summer of 1944 defied conventional military wisdom, but culminated in spectacular success. By January 1945, Patton's forces had reached the German border, capturing thousands of German troops.

Patton was one of the most colorful and controversial figures in military history. Although his outspoken comments and unpredictable actions often were criticized by civilian authorities, he instilled exceptional pride in his men. His toughness earned him the nickname "Old Blood-and-Guts".

"Success is how high you bounce when you hit bottom."

G S Patton Jr.

"By perseverance, study, and eternal desire,
any man can become great."

∽

"Moral courage is the most valuable and usually
the most absent characteristic in men."

∽

"If a man does his best, what else is there?"

∽

"It is only by doing things others have not
that one can advance."

"All glory is fleeting."

"Courage is fear holding on a minute longer."

"Good tactics can save even the worst strategy. Bad tactics will destroy even the best strategy."

"Lead me, follow me, or get out of my way."

"An Army is a team; lives, sleeps, eats, fights as a team."

~

"A man must know his destiny ...
   if he does not recognize it, then he is lost."

Booker T. Washington

1856-1915

Born into slavery in 1856, Booker T. Washington went on to become the most influential black leader and educator of his time. He believed that blacks could benefit more from a practical, vocational education than a college education. His work toward economic prosperity for blacks led to his role as founder and head of Tuskegee Institute, a vocational school for blacks in Tuskegee, Alabama.

The success of Tuskegee Institute as well as Washington's strong belief in mutual progress of blacks and whites made him a shrewd political leader — and an advisor to presidents, congressmen and governors. His autobiography, *Up From Slavery,* was a best-seller that described his rise to national prominence.

In a period of escalating racial tension, Washington's supportive approach was popular with blacks and whites alike. This period became justly known as the "Age of Booker T. Washington".

"There are two ways of exerting one's strength; one is pushing down, the other is pulling up."

"Associate yourself with people of good quality,
for it is better to be alone than in bad company."

⌒

"Character is power."

⌒

"Character, not circumstances, makes the man."

⌒

"Few things can help an individual more than
to place responsibility on him, and to let him
know that you trust him."

"I have learned that success is to be measured not so much by the position that one has reached in life as by the obstacles which he has had to overcome while trying to succeed."

∽

"Nothing ever comes to one, that is worth having, except as a result of hard work."

"One man cannot hold another man down in the ditch without remaining down in the ditch with him."

"There is no power on earth that can neutralize the influence of a high, simple and useful life."

"We must reinforce argument with results."

Theodore Roosevelt

1858–1919

Soldier, statesman, writer and explorer, Theodore Roosevelt became the 26th President of the United States. His enormous energy and zest for life made him one of America's most flamboyant leaders.

Roosevelt served as assistant secretary of the Navy before resigning in 1898 to fight Cuba. Returning as something of a war hero, he easily was elected governor of New York. He then served as Vice President of the United States and took office after McKinley's assassination in 1901.

Roosevelt greatly expanded the powers of the presidency and of the federal government on the side of public interest in conflicts between big business and big labor. He won the Nobel Peace Prize in 1906 for mediating the end of the Russo-Japanese War and promoted the construction of the Panama Canal. A devout naturalist, Roosevelt was responsible for setting aside thousands of acres of land to preserve what is today our national parks and forests.

"Do what you can,
with what you have,
where you are."

Theodore Roosevelt

"Character, in the long run, is the decisive factor in the life of an individual and of nations alike."

~

"I care not what others think of what I do, but I care very much about what I think of what I do! That is character!"

~

"Far and away the best prize that life has to offer is the chance to work hard at work worth doing."

~

"It is hard to fail, but it is worse never to have tried to succeed."

"*Far better is it to dare mighty things, to win glorious triumphs, even though checkered by failure...than to rank with those poor spirits who neither enjoy nor suffer much, because they live in a gray twilight that knows not victory nor defeat.*"

"*Great thoughts speak only to the thoughtful mind, but great actions speak to all mankind.*"

"*In a moment of decision the best thing you can do is the right thing. The worst thing you can do is nothing.*"

"Keep your eyes on the stars, and your feet on the ground."

~

"No man is worth his salt who is not ready at all times to risk his well-being, to risk his body, to risk his life, in a great cause."

~

"People ask the difference between a leader and a boss. The leader leads, and the boss drives."

"Speak softly and carry a big stick; you will go far."

~

*"The only man who never makes a mistake
is the man who never does anything."*

~

*"The best executive is one who has sense enough to pick
good people to do what he wants done, and self-restraint
enough to keep from meddling with them while they do it."*

~

*"To educate a man in mind and not in morals
is to educate a menace to society."*

"*There has never yet been a man in our history who led a life of ease whose name is worth remembering.*"

~

"*The credit belongs to the man who is actually in the arena; whose face is marred by dust and sweat and blood; who strives valiantly; who errs and comes short again and again; who knows the great enthusiasms, the great devotions, and spends himself in a worthy cause/ who at the best knows in the end the triumph of high achievement; and who at the worst, if he fails, at least fails daring greatly.*"

Albert Schweitzer

1875-1965

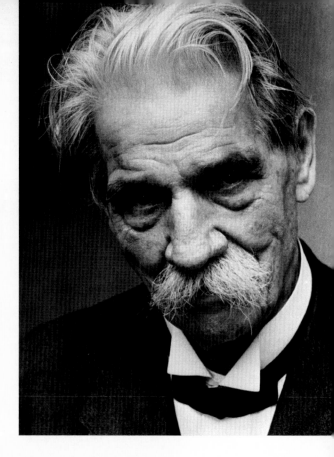

Albert Schweitzer, who has been called one of the greatest Christians of his time, was a brilliant philosopher, musician, theologian and physician.

Schweitzer was born in 1875 in the region of Alsace, Germany. At the age of 21, he decided to devote the next nine years of his life to science, music and preaching. By the time he was 30, he had an international reputation as a writer on theology, a gifted organist, and an authority on the life and works of Johann Sebastian Bach.

While principal of St. Thomas Theological College, he became inspired to become a medical missionary. After studying medicine and surgery for six years, he built his own hospital in Africa. Schweitzer used the proceeds from his concerts and lectures to equip and maintain the hospital. He later set up a leper colony.

Public acknowledgement of his selfless commitment to humanity was bestowed upon him in 1952, when he won the Nobel Peace Prize.

"Success is not the key to happiness.
Happiness is the key to success.
If you love what you are doing,
you will be successful."

Albert Schweitzer

"A great secret of success is to go through life as a man who never gets used up."

꩜

"An optimist is a person who sees a green light everywhere, while the pessimist sees only the red stoplight. The truly wise person is colorblind."

꩜

"As soon as man does not take his existence for granted, but beholds it as something unfathomably mysterious, thought begins."

"Constant kindness can accomplish much. As the sun makes ice melt, kindness causes misunderstanding, mistrust, and hostility to evaporate."

∾

"Do something wonderful, people may imitate it."

∾

"Example is leadership."

∾

"Ethics is nothing else than reverence for life."

"Example is not the main thing
in influencing others.
It is the only thing."

⌒

"I don't know what your destiny
will be, but one thing I know:
the only ones among you who
will be really happy are those
who will have sought and
found how to serve."

"The purpose of human life is to serve, and to
show compassion and the will to help others."

"If a man loses his reverence for any part of life, he will lose his reverence for all of life."

~

"Life becomes harder for us when we live for others, but it also becomes richer and happier."

"One who gains strength by overcoming obstacles possesses the only strength which can overcome adversity."

"The true worth of a man is not to be found in man himself, but in the colours and textures that come alive in others."

"Truth has no special time of its own. Its hour is now — always."

"I can do no other than be reverent before everything that is called life. I can do no other than to have compassion for all that is called life. That is the beginning and the foundation of all ethics."

Sam Walton

1918-1992

A child of the depression, Sam Walton came from humble and hard-working roots. As a pioneering retailer, he made the discount shopping store a phenomenal success in America.

Walton began his retail career in 1940. He and his brother opened the first Wal-Mart discount store in 1962 in Arkansas.

Cutting costs to the absolute maximum and passing the savings onto the customer, along with advanced computerization and automated distribution centers, became the key to success of Wal-Mart. Stores opened across the country and Wal-Mart became the world's largest retailer in 1991.

Today, Sam Walton's empire has grown to over 3,000 stores with sales over $104 billion. His enterprising and innovative dream continues to grow.

"Individuals don't win. Teams do."

"Capital isn't scarce; vision is."

⌇

"Outstanding leaders go out of their way
to boost the self-esteem of their personnel.
If people believe in themselves, it's amazing
what they can accomplish."

⌇

"High expectations are the key to everything."

"I have always been driven to buck the system to innovate, to take things beyond where they've been."

❧

"There is only one boss. The customer. And he can fire everybody in the company from the chairman on down, simply by spending his money somewhere else."

❧

"We let folks know we're interested in them and that they're vital to us, cause they are."

"Appreciate everything your associates do for the business. Nothing else can quite substitute for a few well-chosen, well-timed, sincere words of praise. They're absolutely free and worth a fortune."

Margaret Thatcher

1925-

Margaret Thatcher is the first woman in European history to be elected prime minister.

The daughter of a grocer, she received her degree in chemistry at Oxford, where she became president of the University Conservative Association. During the 1950's, she worked as a research chemist and also studied law, specializing in taxation.

She first ran for Parliament in 1950, but it was not until 1959 that she was finally elected to the House of Commons. She served as parliamentary secretary to the Ministry of Pensions and National Insurance, and later as secretary of state for education and science.

Thatcher was elected the leader of the Conservative Party in 1975, and the party's victory in the 1979 elections elevated her to the office of prime minister.

"You may have to fight a battle more than once to win it."

Margaret A. Thatcher

"Being powerful is like being a lady.
If you have to tell people you are, you aren't."

⌇

"Disciplining yourself to do what you know is right
and important, although difficult, is the highroad
to pride, self-esteem, and personal satisfaction."

⌇

"If you lead a country like Britain, a strong country, a
country which has taken a lead in world affairs in good
times and in bad, a country that is always reliable, then
you have to have a touch of iron about you."

*"Standing in the middle of the road is very dangerous;
you get knocked down by the traffic from both sides."*

~

*"If you set out to be liked, you would be prepared to compromise
on anything at any time, and you would achieve nothing."*

~

*"To wear your heart on your sleeve isn't a very good plan;
you should wear it inside, where it functions best."*

~

*"If my critics saw me walking over the Thames
they would say it was because I couldn't swim."*

"Success is having a flair for the thing that you are doing; knowing that is not enough, that you have got to have hard work and a sense of purpose."

"It pays to know the enemy — not least because at some time you may have the opportunity to turn him into a friend."

"I am in politics because of the conflict between good and evil, and I believe that in the end good will triumph."

Harry S. Truman

1884–1972

The 33rd President of the United States, Harry S. Truman faced the tumultuous years at the close of World War II with the blend of honesty, grit and determination that would make him a modern folk hero.

After serving as a captain in World War I, he became a judge and senator before becoming Vice President. When Franklin D. Roosevelt died in 1945, Truman suddenly was faced with some of the most difficult decisions in U.S. history. In swift order he made final arrangements for the charter-writing meeting of the United Nations, helped arrange Germany's unconditional surrender, attended a summit meeting at Potsdam, and brought an end to the war in the Pacific by using the atomic bomb on Hiroshima and Nagasaki.

Elected in his own right in 1948, he went on to implement the Marshall Plan for economic recovery in Western Europe and to form the North Atlantic Treaty Organization (NATO) pact, a collective security agreement with non-Communist European nations.

"A pessimist is one who makes difficulties of his opportunities and an optimist is one who makes opportunities of his difficulties."

"A President needs political understanding to run the government, but he may be elected without it."

~

"Actions are the seeds of fate. Deeds grow into destiny."

~

"America was not built on fear.
America was built on courage,
on imagination and an unbeatable
determination to do the job at hand."

"I never did give anybody hell. I just told
the truth and they thought it was hell."

＄

"I would rather have peace in the world than be President."

＄

"If you can't convince them, confuse them."

＄

"If you can't stand the heat, get out of the kitchen."

"It is amazing what you can accomplish if you do not care who gets the credit."

~

"It is understanding that gives us an ability to have peace. When we understand the other fellow's viewpoint, and he understands ours, then we can sit down and work out our differences."

"The buck stops here!"

John Wooden

1910-

A keen student of the game and a master motivator, John Wooden was one of the greatest coaches in college basketball history. He led his teams at the University of California at Los Angeles to a record 10 NCAA championships.

As a player at Purdue University, Wooden earned All-America honors in 1930, 1931 and 1932. He coached high school basketball before serving in the U.S. Navy during World War II. After the war, he became head basketball coach and athletic director at Indiana State Teachers' College. He was appointed head coach at UCLA in 1948.

At UCLA, he parlayed the talents of such stars as Lew Alcindor (later Kareem Abdul-Jabbar), Gail Goodrich and Bill Walton into a virtual college basketball dynasty. His teams won a record seven straight NCAA championships from 1967-1973. From 1971 to 1974, UCLA won 88 consecutive games, a college basketball record. John Wooden is the only person named to the Basketball Hall of Fame as both a player and a coach.

"Things turn out best for the people who make the best of the way things turn out."

John Wooden

"Ability is a poor man's wealth."

～

"Be more concerned with your character than your reputation, because your character is what you really are, while your reputation is merely what others think you are."

～

"Adversity is the state in which man most easily becomes acquainted with himself."

～

"Be prepared and be honest."

"Consider the rights of others before your own feelings, and the feelings of others before your own rights."

~

"Do not let what you cannot do interfere with what you can do."

~

"Never mistake activity for achievement."

"Failure is not fatal, but failure to change might be."

*"It's what you learn after
you know it all that counts."*

*"Don't measure yourself by what you have accomplished,
but by what you should have accomplished with your ability."*

*"You can't live a perfect day without
doing something for someone who will
never be able to repay you."*

Andrew Jackson

1767–1845

Born in a log cabin in the wilds of the Carolinas and orphaned at the age of 14, Andrew Jackson grew up with the frontier spirit of one always ready to defend and honor his country. His self-reliance and determination would serve him well as a lawyer, judge, congressman, senator, military hero and the seventh President of the United States.

It was his heroism in the War of 1812 that earned him the nickname "Old Hickory" and thrust him into national prominence. Jackson and his Tennessee militia defeated the British at New Orleans, marking the end of the fighting.

His military triumphs led to his nomination as President, and he was elected in 1828. His election marked the first time a President was elected from the area west of Appalachians and the first time an election focused on direct mass appeal to the voters. This rising tide of democratic sentiment became known as "Jacksonian Democracy".

"One man with courage makes a majority."

Andrew Jackson

"As long as our government is administered for the good of the people, and is regulated by their will; as long as it secures to us the rights of persons and of property, liberty of conscience and of the press, it will be worth defending."

〜

"Any man worth his salt will stick up for what he believes right, but it takes a slightly better man to acknowledge instantly and without reservation that he is in error."

〜

"The brave man inattentive to his duty, is worth little more to his country than the coward who deserts in the hour of danger."

"Every good citizen makes his country's honor his own, and cherishes it not only as precious but as sacred. He is willing to risk his life in its defense and its conscious that he gains protection while he gives it."

"Never take counsel of your fears."

"Peace, above all things, is to be desired,
but blood must sometimes be spilled to
obtain it on equable and lasting terms."

~

"Take time to deliberate;
but when the time for action arrives,
stop thinking and go in."

~

"You must pay the price if you wish
to secure the blessing."

Ray Kroc
1902-1984

As founder of the McDonald's Corporation, Ray A. Kroc largely is responsible for revolutionizing the restaurant industry. His persistence, diligence and faithfulness set the standard for modern business leadership.

Kroc's opportunity for success came in the form of a small restaurant in San Bernardino, California, run by the McDonald brothers. Their assembly-line method of serving hamburgers, french fries and milk shakes was simple but efficient. Kroc knew that this concept would have a great appeal to consumers.

The first of Kroc's McDonald's was opened April 15, 1955. Kroc continued to expand by introducing a unique franchise system. His methods and ideas about customer service have served as models for many different industries.

Kroc's steadfast devotion to an idea brought him personal success, and also allowed him to set up several charities and educational organizations.

"Luck is a dividend of sweat. The more you sweat, the luckier you get."

"Are you green and growing or ripe and rotting?"

∽

"If you work just for money, you'll never make it,
but if you love what you're doing and you always
put the customer first, success will be yours."

∽

"If you're not a risk taker,
you should get out of business."

Golda Meir
1898-1978

Golda Meir was a founder of the State of Israel and served as its fourth prime minister (1969-74). Born in Kiev, the Ukraine, in 1898, she emigrated to Wisconsin in 1906. Her political activity began as a leader in the Milwaukee Labor Zionist Party.

After emigrating to Palestine in 1921, she held key posts in the Jewish Agency and in the World Zionist Organization. After Israel proclaimed its independence in 1948, she served as minister of labor and then foreign minister. She was appointed prime minister in 1969.

During her administration, she worked for a peace settlement in the Middle East using diplomatic means. Her efforts at forging peace were halted by the outbreak of the fourth Arab-Israeli War. She resigned her post in 1974 but remained an important political figure throughout her retirement. Her true strength and spirit were emphasized when, after her death in 1978, it was revealed that she had suffered from leukemia for 12 years.

"One cannot and must not try to erase the past merely because it does not fit the present."

Golda Meir

"The only alternative to war is peace.
The only road to peace is negotiation."

〜

"You'll never find a better sparring partner than adversity."

〜

"Trust yourself. Create the kind of self
that you will be happy to live with
all of your life. Make the most of
yourself by fanning the tiny, inner sparks
of possibility into flames of achievement."

Douglas MacArthur

1880-1964

Douglas MacArthur graduated from West Point with the highest honors in his class. Brilliant and controversial, he carried his ambition and lust for achievement through posts in World War I, World War II, and the Korean War.

During the course of World War I, MacArthur was promoted to full general and became army chief of staff. MacArthur battled the Japanese in the Philippines during World War II, and served as Allied commander of the Japanese occupation.

The Korean War began in 1950, and MacArthur was soon selected to command United Nations forces there. After initial success, he then encountered massive Chinese resistance and entered into a bitter dispute with President Truman. Despite Truman's insistence on a limited war, MacArthur persisted in initiating the offensive. He was relieved of command by Truman for insubordination in 1951. Ever aloof and enigmatic, MacArthur retired to private life, the symbol of zealous dedication to duty, honor and country.

"There is no substitute for victory."

Douglas MacArthur

"Nobody grows old by merely living a number of years.
People grow old by deserting their ideals.
You are as young as your faith, as old as your doubt;
as young your self-confidence, as old as your fear;
as young as your hope, as old as your despair."

~

"You are remembered for the rules you break."

~

"Moral courage, the courage of one's convictions,
the courage to see things through the eyes of the world —
is in a constant conspiracy against the brave.
It is the age old struggle — the roar of the crowd on one side
and the voice of your conscience on the other."

www.simpletruths.com